Visit Egypt!

Jill Laidlaw

Crabtree Publishing Company
www.crabtreebooks.com

Author: Jill Laidlaw
Editor: Crystal Sikkens
Project coordinator: Kathy Middleton
Production coordinator: Ken Wright
Prepress technician: Margaret Amy Salter
Series consultant: Gill Matthews

Picture credits:
Corbis: The Art Archive 14, The Gallery Collection 11,
  Mike Nelson/epa 13, Roger Wood 15
Dreamstime: Mahmoudmahdy 7
Fotolia: Cambo 16
Istockphoto: (Cover) Ben McLeish, Karim Hesham 6,
Rex Features: Quilici / Iverson 12
Shutterstock: (Cover), Vaju Ariel 21, WH Chow 5,
  Mirek Hejnicki 19, André Klaassen 20, Michal Kram 9,
  Mary Lane 8, Bill McKelvie 17, Marco_tb 10,
  Styve Reineck 18
Map: Geoff Ward 4

Every effort has been made to trace copyright holders and to obtain their permission for use of copyright material. The authors and publishers would be pleased to rectify any error or omission in future editions. All the Internet addresses given in this book were correct at the time of going to press. The author and publishers regret any inconvenience caused if addresses have changed or sites have ceased to exist, but can accept no responsibility for any such changes.

Library and Archives Canada Cataloguing in Publication

Laidlaw, Jill A.
  Visit Egypt! / Jill Laidlaw.

(Crabtree connections)
Includes index.
ISBN 978-0-7787-9956-6 (bound).--ISBN 978-0-7787-9978-8 (pbk)

  1. Egypt--Juvenile literature. 2. Egypt--Description and
travel--Juvenile literature. 3. Egypt--Antiquities--Guidebooks--
Juvenile literature. I. Title. II. Series: Crabtree connections.

DT49.L29 2010   j962   C2010-901516-9

Library of Congress Cataloging-in-Publication Data

Laidlaw, Jill A.
  Visit Egypt! / Jill Laidlaw.
    p. cm. -- (Crabtree connections)
  Includes index.
  ISBN 978-0-7787-9956-6 (reinforced lib. bdg. : alk. paper)
  -- ISBN 978-0-7787-9978-8 (pbk. : alk. paper)
  1. Egypt--Juvenile literature. 2. Egypt--Civilization--To 332 B.C.
--Juvenile literature. I. Title. II. Series.

DT49.L274 2010
932--dc22
                                        2010008069

Crabtree Publishing Company

www.crabtreebooks.com   1-800-387-7650

Printed in the U.S.A./062010/WO20100815

Published in Canada
Crabtree Publishing
616 Welland Ave.
St. Catharines, Ontario
L2M 5V6

Published in the United States
Crabtree Publishing
PMB 59051
350 Fifth Avenue, 59th Floor
New York, New York 10118

Contents

Land of Sun

Welcome to the Arab Republic of Egypt in northern Africa. What do you think you will see here? Egypt is a country of contrasts. You can find deserts next to rich farmland. Ancient pyramids can be seen from modern skyscraper hotels.

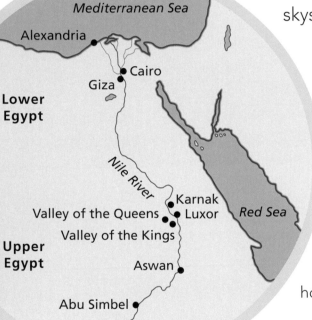

This map of Egypt shows some of the main sites to visit.

Getting here

The easiest and quickest way to get to Egypt is by airplane. The cities of Cairo, Luxor, and Aswan all have modern airports. Once you are here you can travel from city to city by air, rail, or road. We also have camels, hot-air balloons, horse-drawn taxis, and sailboats.

Year-round Sun

Egypt is the perfect holiday destination for anyone who enjoys the heat. We have two seasons—winter and summer. Winter is from October/November to March. The temperature stays between 52°F (11°C) and 64°F (18°C). Summer is from April to September/October. From June to July, the average temperature is 84°F (29°C), but it can rise to 122°F (50°C)!

The Nile Valley

Come to the Nile Valley. This is where the ancient Egyptians built many pyramids and temples.

You can see:
- the Great Pyramid at Giza
- temples at Luxor and Karnak
- the Valley of the Kings
- the Valley of the Queens
- mortuary temples of the dead
- the temples of Abu Simbel

Travel Tip

The tourist season in Egypt is during the winter. The cooler air makes it more comfortable for sightseeing.

The Nile River is the main highway of Egypt. It is also the world's longest river. Take a cruise along the Nile. You will see over 5,000 years of history in one week.

Traditional boats, called *feluccas*, travel along the Nile.

The Biggest Pyramid on Earth

Catch a ride to Giza, on the outskirts of Cairo, to see the pyramids. You must visit the Great Pyramid. It is the biggest pyramid in Egypt. It was built for Pharaoh Khufu, who ruled from around 2551 to 2528 BC. That was just over 4,500 years ago.

The Great Pyramid is made of around 2 million blocks of limestone.

Dark tunnels

I hope you are not afraid of small spaces. The entrance to the Great Pyramid is a narrow, low corridor. It is very dark, hot, and cramped. The corridor plunges down into the pyramid, leading to an unfinished chamber. Next, move into a small tunnel and climb upward. This will take you to the Queen's Chamber.

Did you know?

The base of the Great Pyramid is as big as eight soccer fields.

Grave robbers

From the Queen's Chamber, climb higher into the Grand Gallery. It is a huge space—154 feet (47 m) long, and the roof hovers 26 feet (8 m) above your head.

Now climb beyond the Gallery to the King's Chamber. This is the heart of the pyramid. Here you will see Khufu's **sarcophagus**. Grave robbers stole everything else centuries ago. The sarcophagus is made of red stone called granite. It was too heavy to lift so the robbers had to leave it!

🧳 Travel Tip

Drink a lot of water—if you don't you may get sick because of the heat.

The pyramids at Giza are guarded by a huge **sphinx**.

7

Temples of the Gods

Once you have seen the Great Pyramid, take a boat down the Nile River to see two of our finest temple sites.

Luxor Temple

The modern town of Luxor was built on top of Thebes, which was the capital of Egypt around 1991 BC. The Temple of Luxor sits near the waterfront on the east bank of the Nile.

The columns inside Luxor Temple are decorated with beautiful paintings.

Past times

- King Amemhotep III reigned from about 1402 to 1364 BC. He started Luxor Temple and dedicated it to the gods **Amun-Ra**, **Mut**, and **Khonsu**.

- The ancient Egyptians left Thebes, and it became covered by the sand of the desert. It was buried and forgotten for thousands of years.

- Luxor Temple was rediscovered in 1885 AD. The buildings that surrounded it were cleared away to reveal the ancient temple.

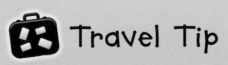 Travel Tip

There's a light and sound show at Karnak. It displays all Karnak's magnificent history in a fun way, three times a night during the tourist season.

Karnak

The largest surviving ancient religious site in the world is at Karnak. It is near Luxor.

The Precinct of Amun

The temple complex at Karnak has different parts, called precincts. These contain many temples—there's enough room here for ten cathedrals.

Some of the things you can see in the Precinct of Amun include:

- A walkway of splendid sphinxes with the bodies of lions and the heads of rams

- "Pylons" or temple gateways. The first pylon you come to is 141 feet (43 m) high—the tallest pylon in Egypt

- The Temple of **Rameses II**— one of the most famous pharaohs of ancient Egypt

- Two massive statues, called *colossi*, of Rameses II

- The Great Hypostyle Hall—a hall of 140 huge stone pillars

This limestone statue stands at the Temple of Amun at Karnak.

The Valley of the Kings

The Valley of the Kings is the graveyard of the pharaohs. It takes up an entire valley. The pyramids kept being robbed, so they buried the pharaohs in the Valley of the Kings in tombs cut deep into the rock. But the tombs were also robbed.

How to get there

The Valley of the Kings is across from Luxor, on the west bank of the Nile River. You can ride a ferry across the river and then take a taxi or rent a bicycle.

Which valley?

The area is split into two—the east valley and the west valley. Most tourists visit the east valley—there are a lot of tombs to see, including that of Tutankhamun. The west valley has only one tomb open to the public.

🧳 Travel Tip

You must buy tickets to go into the tombs. You need to buy a separate ticket for Tutankhamun's tomb.

This is the entrance to Tutankhamun's tomb.

Tomb entry

How many tombs do you think you could see in one day? Probably only about three or four. Not all of the tombs are open—some are closed for study, and some are kept closed to protect them.

This is a painting of Pharaoh Rameses II. His tomb is found in the Valley of the Kings.

Top four tombs

- The tomb of Rameses IV has been a tourist attraction for thousands of years.

- The tomb of Tutankhamun is the most famous tomb in the valley. See pages 12–13.

- The tomb of the sons of Rameses II is thought to have about 120 rooms!

- The tomb of **Tuthmosis III** is one of the oldest in the valley.

Tutankhamun

In the heart of the Valley of the Kings is the tomb of Tutankhamun—the most famous pharaoh in the world. He was crowned ruler of Egypt when he was only nine years old and died at the age of 19 or 20.

Tutankhamun's tomb is very small. This is because he wasn't a very important pharaoh. His tomb was discovered in 1922 with most of its treasures still safe inside.

Tutankhamun's body was found inside a huge stone sarcophagus.

Was the king murdered?

Tutankhamun died very suddenly and was buried in a hurry—you can tell by looking at the pictures on the tomb walls. Paint has been splashed on some of them as if they were finished in a rush. No one knows how Tutankhamun died. Some people think he was murdered. Some people think he broke his leg, perhaps in a chariot accident, and died afterward from the infected wound.

Treasures

Some of the treasures found in Tutankhamun's tomb were:

- Eight baskets of 3,000-year-old fruit
- A solid gold mask, which was placed on his face after his death (see page 21)

Look at the face of Tutankhamun inside his burial chamber.

The face of a pharaoh

You can see Tutankhamun for yourself when you go into his burial chamber. Remember to be quiet to show your respect for the person who is buried here. Tutankhamun's body is wrapped in linen and is on display in a glass box. You can even see his face. The temperature inside the box is controlled by a computer to stop the mummy from decaying.

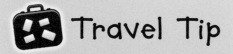 Travel Tip

Go to the Egyptian Museum in Cairo to see the artifacts that were in Tutankhamun's tomb (see pages 20–21).

The Valley of the Queens

It's not just pharaohs who are buried in the Valley of the Kings. Nobles, royal wives, and children are buried there, too.

Around 1300 BC, work started on the Valley of the Queens near the Valley of the Kings. This was to be a separate place for wives to be buried. But some wives were still buried with their husbands in the Valley of the Kings.

Despite being thousands of years old, this wall painting from **Nefertari's** tomb is still very bright.

Less space

Many of the tombs in the Valley of the Queens were built to the same basic plan as the tombs in the Valley of the Kings—they are just smaller. They each have an entrance, a corridor, a few rooms, and a burial chamber.

Did you know?

There are more than 80 tombs in the Valley of the Queens. Most of them are closed to the public. You can only visit four tombs.

Nefertari

The most famous tomb in the Valley of the Queens belongs to Nefertari—the favorite wife of pharaoh Rameses II. Nefertari's tomb is the biggest in the valley. The wall paintings in this tomb are beautiful, but very fragile.

Paintings of Nefertari decorate the walls of her tomb.

Be warned!

- Only 150 people are allowed to visit Nefertari's tomb each day—so show up early.

- You'll have to wear a mask because your breath can damage the paintings.

- You'll have to wear shoe covers to stop dust from coming into the tomb and causing more damage.

🧳 Travel Tip

You are not allowed to take photographs in the tombs. Flash photography can harm the paintings. Leave your camera at the door.

Temples of the Dead

The ancient Egyptians didn't just build temples to the gods—they also built temples to worship dead pharaohs. These temples are called mortuary temples. There are many mortuary temples near the Valley of the Kings. Most of them are in ruins.

Hatshepsut's temple

The most beautiful temple of all belongs to Hatshepsut, the wife of **Tuthmosis II**. When her husband died, Hatshepsut decided to rule Egypt instead of her nephew, who was next in line to the throne. She ruled from 1490 to 1468 BC. You can visit the three floors of Hatshepsut's temple—the bottom two floors would have been filled with trees and perfumed fountains.

Smashed to pieces

When Hatshepsut's nephew, Tuthmosis III, finally came to the throne, he gave orders for all the buildings Hatshepsut created to be destroyed, including her temple. **Egyptologists** have been slowly restoring Hatshepsut's temple—sometimes rebuilding a statue or a wall from thousands of pieces of stone.

The terraces of Queen Hatshepsut's temple can still be clearly seen today.

The ghost village

A walled village, called Deir al Madina, lies behind the mortuary temples. The village is now empty, but once it was home to the best craftsmen in Egypt. They worked on the surrounding tombs and temples. The craftsmen were kept away from other people so that they couldn't tell anyone where the pharaohs' tombs could be found.

Hatshepsut wore a false beard to make her look like a male pharaoh.

🧳 Travel Tip

Modern Egypt is a Muslim country. Tourists should always wear sensible, respectful clothes when visiting pyramids, temples, and ancient sites.

The World's Biggest Jigsaw

In 1964, the Egyptian government decided to build a dam across the Nile River at a place called Aswan. Building the dam would flood the temples at nearby Abu Simbel. So the temples were cut into 1,036 pieces and moved 196 feet (60 m) higher up the cliff to be safe from the water. They were then put back together again like a giant jigsaw puzzle.

Getting there

The best way to get to Abu Simbel is by boat. River trips leave Cairo for Aswan every week.

Temples of Rameses II

Around 1257 BC, the great Pharaoh Rameses II ordered his workmen to cut two temples out of the rock on the west bank of the Nile, just south of Aswan. One of the temples was for himself and the other was for his favorite wife, Nefertari.

The walls of Abu Simbel are carved with images of ancient Egypt.

Hypostyle Hall

The biggest chamber is called the Hypostyle Hall. It has eight 32 foot (10 m) tall statues of Rameses II dressed as the god Osiris, ruler of the dead.

As you move into the cliff, the rooms become smaller and smaller until you reach the "sanctuary." This is a room that contains the statues of Rameses II and Amun-Ra, **Ra-Horakhte**, and **Ptah**—the gods the temple is dedicated to.

Travel Tip

Try some of the local food when you visit Aswan. Vine leaves stuffed with spiced meat, roast pigeon, and kabobs are all very popular.

Four statues of Rameses II sit outside the entrance to his temple.

A Place of Wonders

When you are in Cairo you must visit the Egyptian Museum in Tahrir Square. It has the most wonderful collection of ancient Egyptian objects in the world. About 7,000 people visit the museum every day.

What's inside?

There are nearly 90 rooms spread over two floors in the Egyptian Museum. You can see:

- coins
- sculptures
- coffins
- jewelry
- chariots
- musical instruments
- children's games
- boats
- mummies
- weapons

The oldest objects are on the ground floor. Walking around is like taking a walk through ancient Egypt itself.

The Egyptian Museum in Cairo is lit up at night.

About 3,500 objects from Tutankhamun's tomb are on display in the museum, including his death mask (shown above).

Amazing articles

In the museum you will find:

- The mummies of 11 pharaohs

- The mummy of Rameses II. This pharaoh's body is well preserved. He still has skin, teeth, and hair

- The solid gold mask of Tutankhamun

Every month the museum staff chooses one special object to put on display.

Be quiet!

When you go into the room that has the mummies of pharaohs in it, you will be asked to keep quiet out of respect for the dead people in the room.

🧳 Travel Tip

Take a lot of water. The museum is not air-conditioned and can get very hot!

Did you know?

The Egyptian Museum has so many objects that if you spent one minute looking at every single one of them, it would take nine months to see them all!

Glossary

Amun-Ra Amun-Ra was half god of Thebes (the ancient capital of Egypt) and half Sun god. He was shown as having the body of a man and the head of a ram

Egyptologists The name given to people who study ancient Egyptian history at any point between the fifth century BC and the fourth century AD

Khonsu The Moon god, a god of the sky. He is shown as a human with a falcon head and wears a large circle, like the Moon

Mut Wife of Amun-Ra. Mut was the mother goddess and the queen of all living things. She is often shown as a woman wearing a vulture headdress

Nefertari (c. 1300–1250 BC) The "Royal" or "Chief" queen of Pharaoh Rameses II. Nefertari married Rameses II when she was 13 and he was 15

Ptah The god of architects and artists. Ptah created the plan for the universe. He looked like a man wrapped in white cloth and carried a long staff or stick

Ra-Horakhte He was half Sun god Ra and half falcon god Horus, who was god of the sky

Rameses II (c.1289–1224 BC) One of the most famous pharaohs of ancient Egypt. Rameses built a lot of monuments, such as the two temples at Abu Simbel

sarcophagus The outer coffin left above ground. In ancient Egypt, there could be several coffins inside the sarcophagus, so it could be very large

sphinx Stone statue of a lion with the head of a man or woman

Tuthmosis II Came to the throne of Egypt after the death of his father, Tuthmosis I. He was a weak pharaoh

Tuthmosis III (c.1490–1436 BC) The son of Tuthmosis II and the nephew of Hatshepsut. As pharaoh, Tuthmosis III became a great warrior king

Further Information

Web sites

The Web site of the Egyptian Tourism office is full of information about the opening times of museums and pyramids, Nile River cruises, hotels, and tours. Visit it at: **www.egypt.travel**

Find out about life in ancient Egypt—everything from arts and architecture to gods and government—at: **www.historyforkids.org/learn/egypt/**

Try these exciting online activities and games to find out more about the ancient world of the Egyptians: **library.thinkquest.org/CR0210200/ancient_egypt/ online_activities.htm**

Books

Ancient Egypt by George Hart. DK Publishing (2008)

The Egyptians by Anita Ganeri. Stargazer Books (2010)

Gods and Goddesses of Ancient Egypt by Janeen Adil. Capstone Press (2008)

Life in Ancient Egypt by Paul Challen. Crabtree Publishing Company (2005)

Index